A New Job for Pearl

Illustrated by:
Connie Forslind's 2nd Grade Class
Rancho Romero School

Story Written by:
Allyn Lee

Anastasia Uhland

Dogs also have the wonderful ability to make people smile. When we are sad, petting a dog helps us feel better. Therapy dogs love their job of bringing happiness to people in hospitals.

Anastasia Uhland

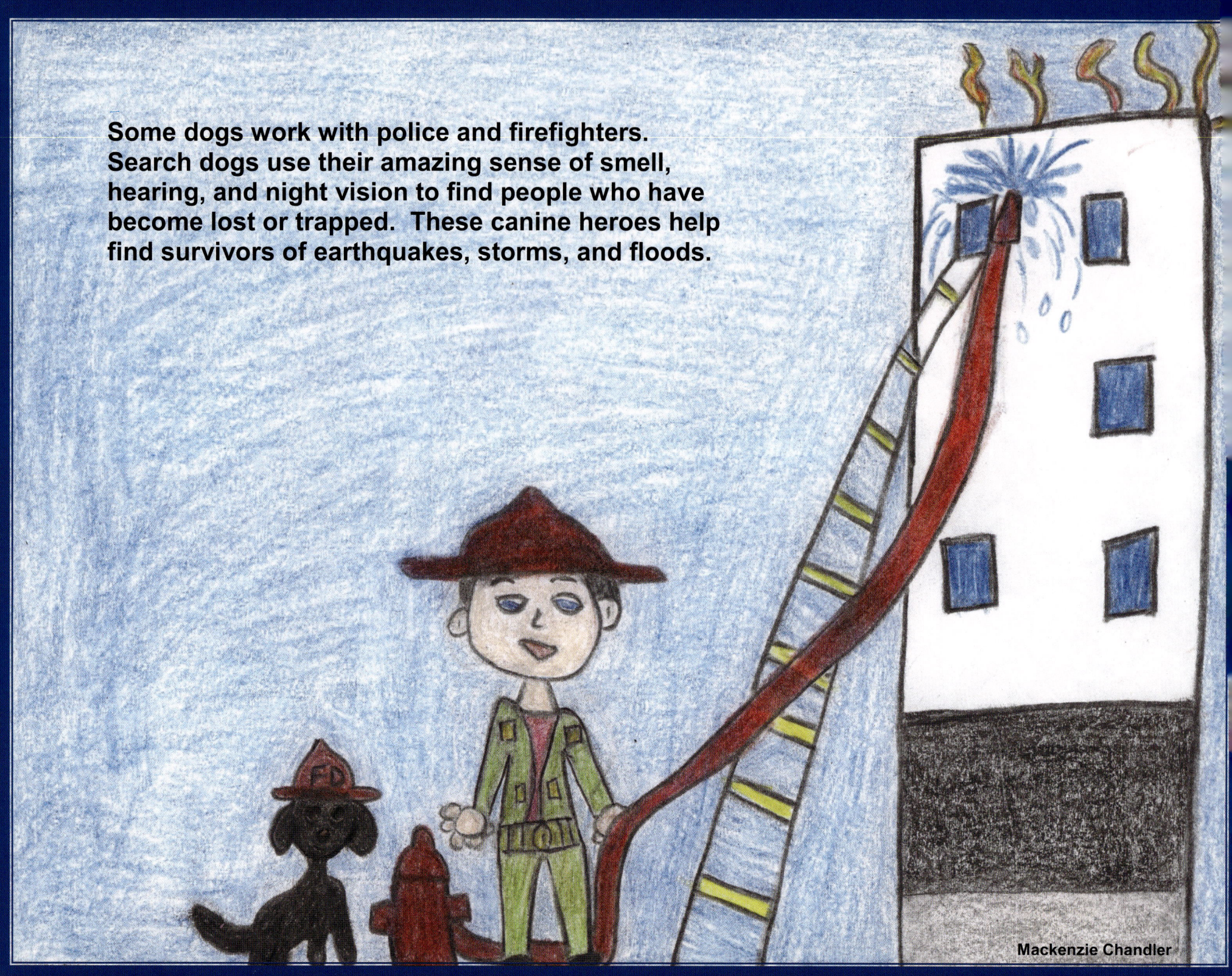

Some dogs work with police and firefighters. Search dogs use their amazing sense of smell, hearing, and night vision to find people who have become lost or trapped. These canine heroes help find survivors of earthquakes, storms, and floods.

Mackenzie Chandler

This is the true story of a once-homeless dog that became part of a search and rescue team. Pearl is a black Labrador Retriever with bright eyes, a smiling face, and a tail that will not stay still. At the beginning of our story, Pearl was a playful and curious two-year-old pup. This big bundle of energy was always looking for an adventure.

Megan Williams

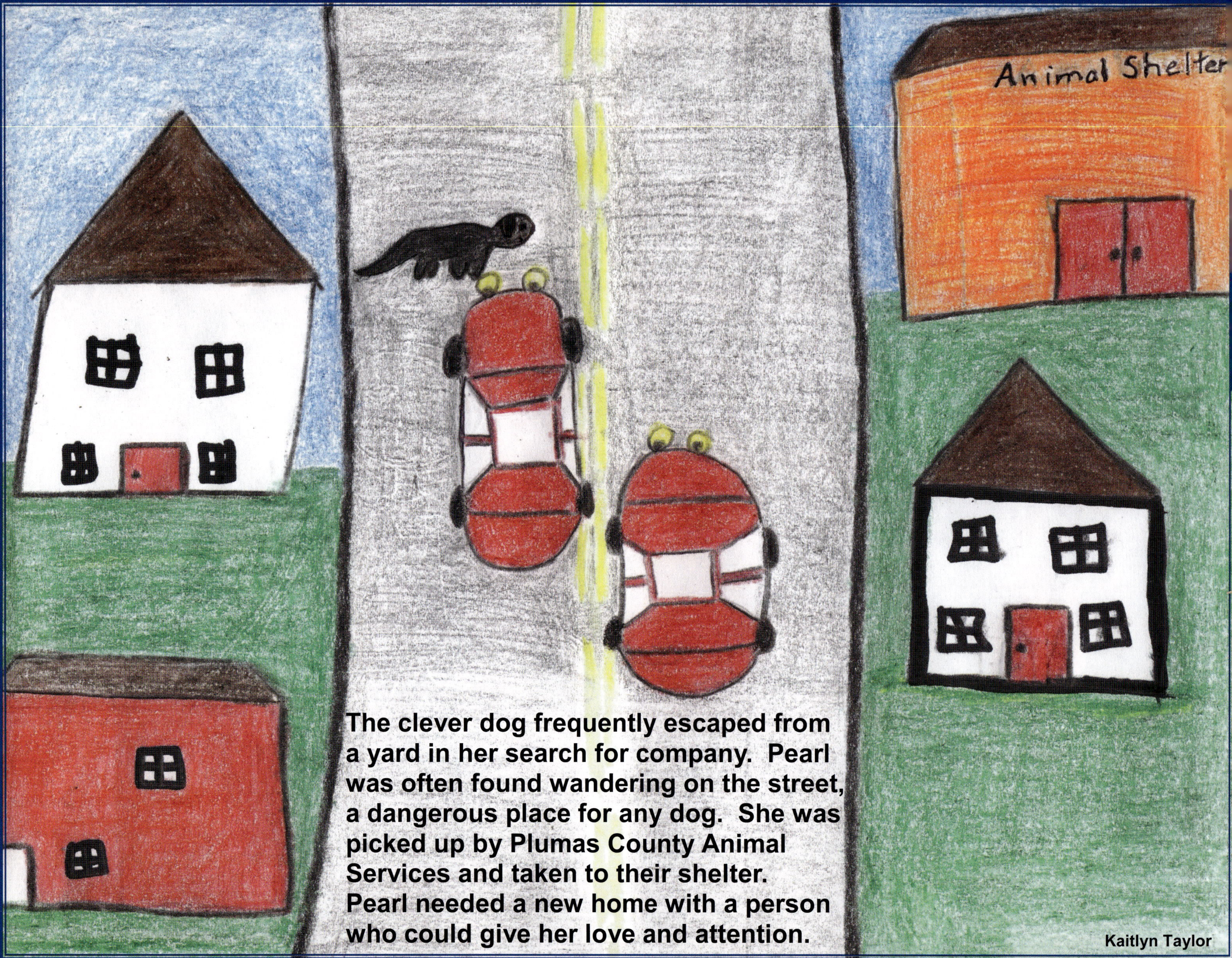

The clever dog frequently escaped from a yard in her search for company. Pearl was often found wandering on the street, a dangerous place for any dog. She was picked up by Plumas County Animal Services and taken to their shelter. Pearl needed a new home with a person who could give her love and attention.

Kaitlyn Taylor

Luckily for Pearl, a member of the Search Dog Foundation "Bark Force" discovered her at High Sierra Animal Rescue. Bark Force team members search animal shelters for dogs that have the qualities for search and rescue work. They look for dogs that need a job.

Emma Cochran

Most people do not enjoy tests, but Pearl thought they were great fun! She easily passed the personality test because she was playful and eager to please. She showed that she was not frightened by sudden movements and loud sounds.

John Sweeney

When it was time for the two most important tests, Pearl was ready for the challenge.
She was a champ at tug-of-war, but her favorite game was retrieving. The trainer threw a toy into thick bushes and Pearl ran to find it. Pearl would not stop until she found and retrieved the toy. She wriggled with excitement while waiting for another toss!

Scott Jin

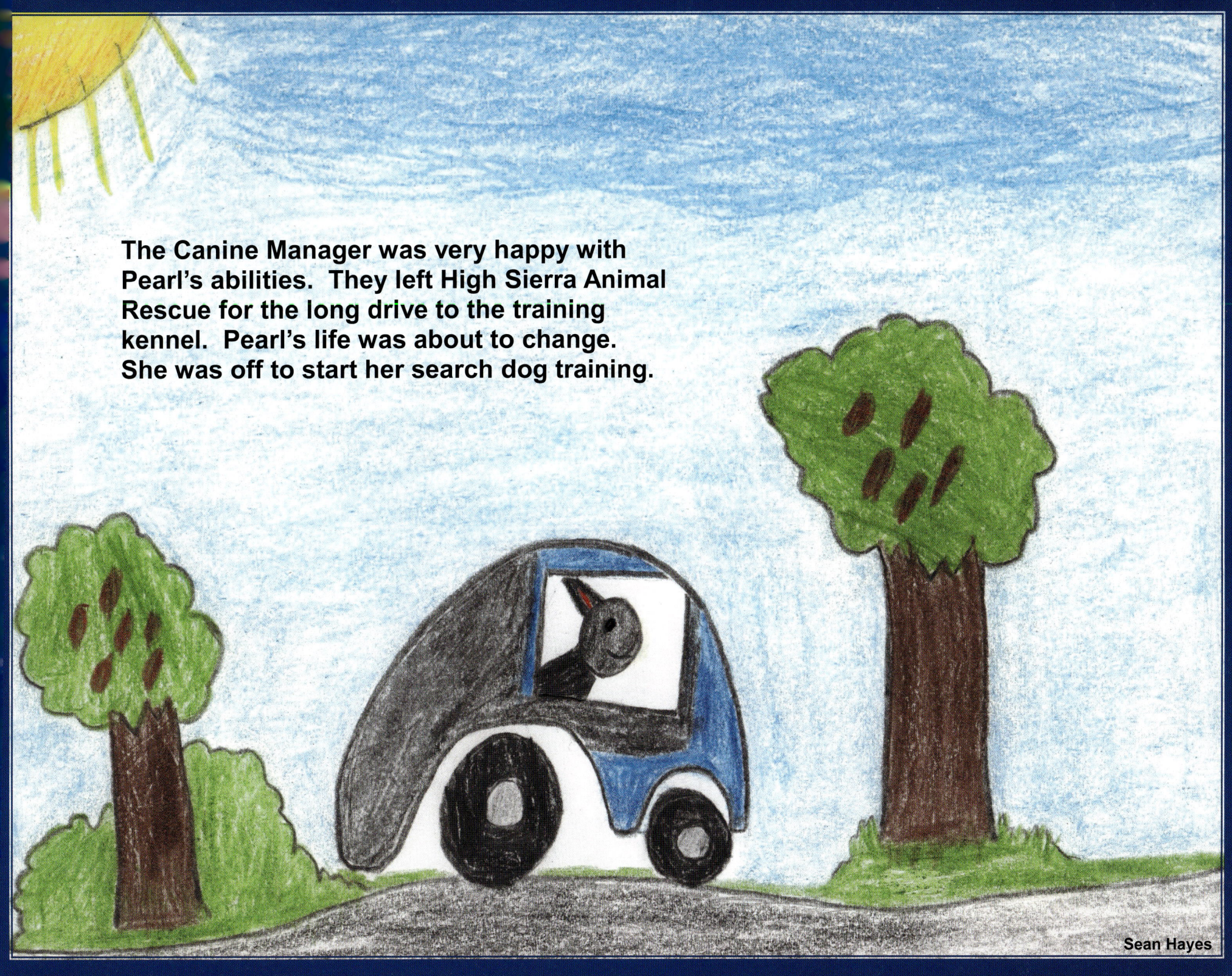

The Canine Manager was very happy with Pearl's abilities. They left High Sierra Animal Rescue for the long drive to the training kennel. Pearl's life was about to change. She was off to start her search dog training.

Sean Hayes

With every day of training, Pearl gained new skills. The agile dog learned to walk carefully through difficult obstacle courses. She had to run over piles of broken concrete and crawl into small spaces. Pearl even learned to climb a ladder!

Makenna Curran

Pearl had a natural eagerness to find a hidden toy. The trainers used her love of hide-and-seek to teach her to find people. Pearl had to concentrate on the search, but the trainers made sure that the work was fun for this playful dog. She was always rewarded with praise and her toy.

Jaden Dow

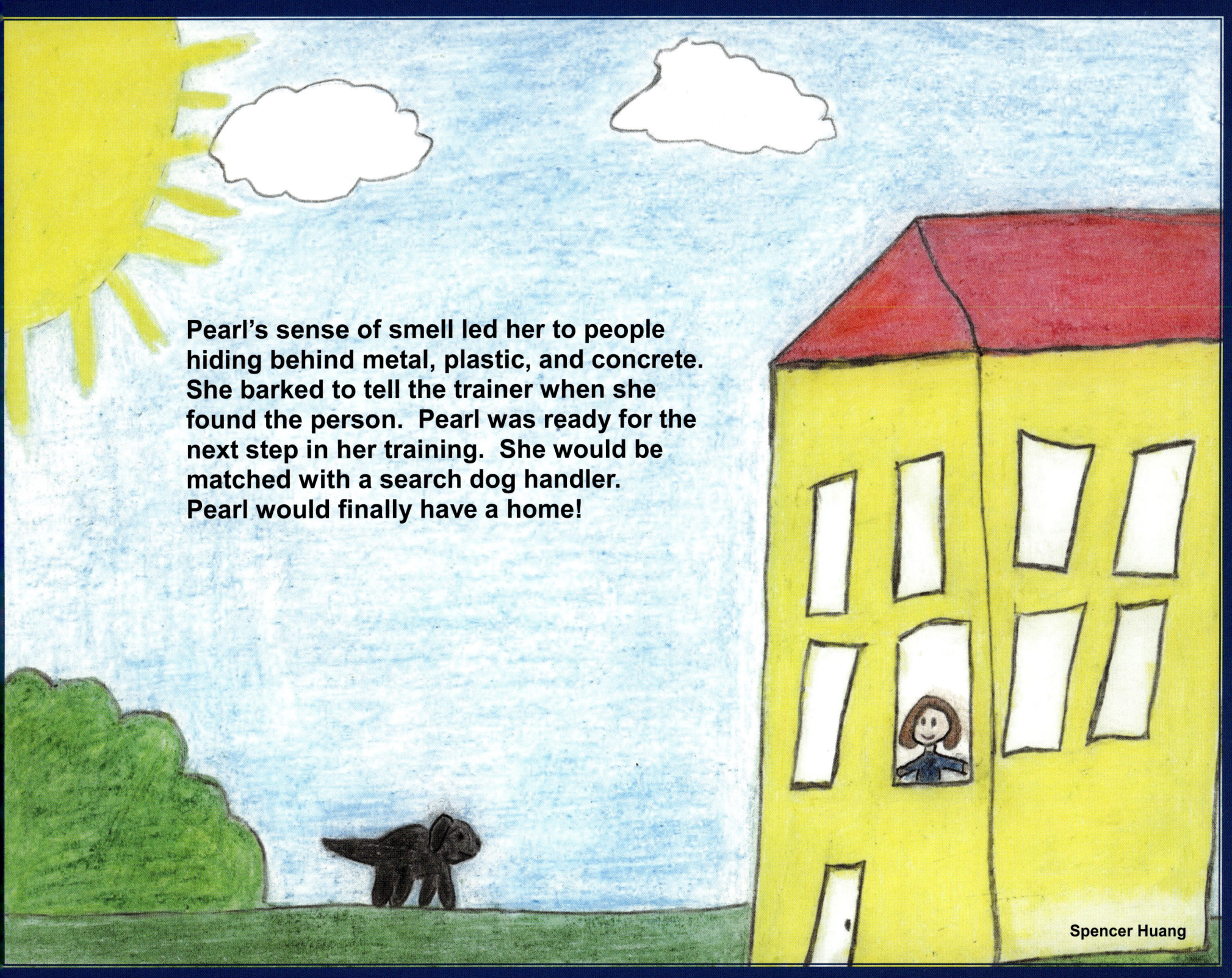

Pearl's sense of smell led her to people hiding behind metal, plastic, and concrete. She barked to tell the trainer when she found the person. Pearl was ready for the next step in her training. She would be matched with a search dog handler. Pearl would finally have a home!

Spencer Huang

This is where our other hero enters the story.
The National Disaster Search Dog Foundation taught
Captain Ron Horetski how to handle trained search dogs.
When he met Pearl, Captain Horetski knew that he had
found a friend *and* a partner. Pearl lives with Captain Horetski
and goes to work with him each day at the fire station.

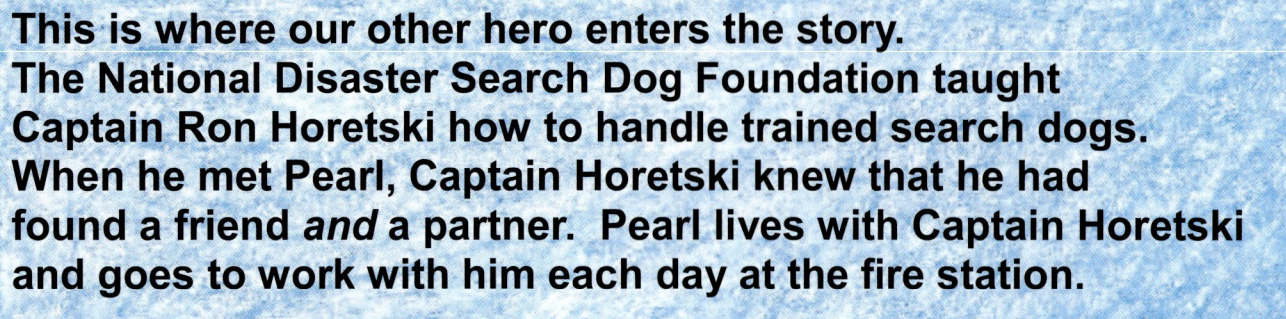

Connor Buchanan

The Daily News

Pearl: a Homeless dog becomes a Hero!

Luke Tyler

Captain Horetski and Pearl flew to Haiti within days of a powerful earthquake. They are part of the California Task Force 2 team that worked to rescue people from collapsed buildings. The conditions were difficult and dangerous, but our hero Pearl never hesitated in her job of finding people in the rubble.

Through the National Disaster Search Dog Foundation, Pearl found a new home *and* a new job!

SEARCH DOG FOUNDATION
Be Part of the Search®

Since its founding in 1996, SDF has rescued hundreds of dogs, many on the brink of euthanasia. They have trained 105 Search Teams, 72 of which are currently active. SDF Teams have been deployed to 66 disasters including the World Trade Center attacks and Hurricane Katrina and state and local emergencies such as earthquakes, mudslides, building collapses, train derailments, and missing person searches. Eight of SDF's teams are members of CA-TF2 and are ready at all times for immediate deployment overseas when called upon by the Office of Foreign Disaster Assistance.

Recent major earthquakes around the world underscore the importance of canine search teams. FEMA Urban Search and Rescue teams join international teams in the effort to help survivors.

Pearl's Photo Album

California Task Force 2

Pearl and Captain Horetski searching in Haiti

Acknowledgements

We are sincerely grateful to People & Properties Sotheby's International Realty for their generous contributions toward *A New Job for Pearl*.

Our story could not be shared without the wonderful work of our desktop publisher and editor, Christine Reder.

Thank you to our talented photographer, Carolyn Uhland.

We thank Lydia Leveriza at Diablo Printing & Copying for her efforts in the beautiful production of our book.

424 DIABLO ROAD · DANVILLE, CA 94526
(925) 743-9090 · FAX: (925) 743-9059
LYDIA@DIABLOPRINTING.COM

Emma Cochran